Mathematics and Computing/Technology
An Inter-faculty Second Level Course

MT262 Putting Computer Systems to Work

Block I
Beginnings

Unit 4
Further Considerations

Prepared for the Course Team by Alan Best

This text forms part of the Open University second-level course MT262 *Putting Computer Systems to Work*, which among other things teaches the use of Borland C^{++}Builder 5 Standard to tackle small programming projects. (Borland C^{++}Builder 5 Standard is copyright © 2000 Borland International (UK) Limited.)

The course software comprises the Borland C^{++}Builder 5 Standard CD-ROM and the MT262 Templates and Libraries CD-ROM, both of which are supplied as part of the course.

This publication forms part of an Open University course. Details of this and other Open University courses can be obtained from the Student Registration and Enquiry Service, The Open University, PO Box 197, Milton Keynes, MK7 6BJ, United Kingdom: tel. +44 (0)870 333 4340, e-mail general-enquiries@open.ac.uk

Alternatively, you may visit the Open University website at http://www.open.ac.uk where you can learn more about the wide range of courses and packs offered at all levels by The Open University.

To purchase a selection of Open University course materials, visit the webshop at www.ouw.co.uk, or contact Open University Worldwide, Michael Young Building, Walton Hall, Milton Keynes, MK7 6AA, United Kingdom, for a brochure: tel. +44 (0)1908 858785, fax +44 (0)1908 858787, e-mail ouwenq@open.ac.uk

The Open University, Walton Hall, Milton Keynes, MK7 6AA.

First published 1999. Second edition 2002.

Edited, designed and typeset by The Open University, using the Open University T$_{\mathrm{E}}$X System.

Printed in the United Kingdom by Martins the Printers, Berwick-upon-Tweed

ISBN 0 7492 4055 5

2.2

Contents

Study guide

The main purpose of this end-of-block unit is to enable you to review, and thereby consolidate, the important ideas of this block. There are very few new ideas introduced, although the tidying up of some loose ends does introduce some further design considerations. Even so, you should find that you can work relatively quickly through this unit, thus giving you time to complete the Assignment for Block I by the date specified on the Study Calendar for the course.

Sections 1 and 2 each require a good deal of involvement with your computer, but the activities are principally demonstrative and so should not take up a great deal of time. Although Subsection 2.3 has no numbered Computer Activities, you will need your computer for that subsection.

Section 3 is a brisk review of key ideas from the block and contains a number of revision exercises.

A suggested study pattern for this unit is as follows.

Material	Study time
Introduction, Section 1 (computer)	2 hours
Section 2 (computer)	2 hours
Section 3 (text)	2 hours

You will need to have *Units 2* and *3* to hand whilst studying this unit.

Introduction

Units 2 and *3* of this block concentrated on reaching a design solution to a problem and then implementing the solution in C++. There are other aspects of the problem solving process that have been largely overlooked. Computing problems invariably work with data, and the solution to a problem cannot be an algorithm to manipulate data alone; it has to involve collation of the data (possibly in physical form — for example, paper records), input of the data to the program, and output of the results. The data to be input presents huge difficulties in problem solving since mistakes can be made during collation of data and during input to the machine. A good solution to a problem would be able to recover from such errors.

You have seen, during the few examples covered in this block, that it is easy to feel confident that a design is 'correct', only to discover flaws when the program is run. The first program discussed in detail, to calculate the mean of four whole numbers, looked fine until features were discovered about how the machine handles integer division. A common error made by programmers is to reach a solution which works *for most cases* but can fall over in exceptional cases. For instance, a program which requires the user to input a string value might work perfectly until the user enters, accidentally or otherwise, the null (or empty) string. A robust program has to handle such extreme situations; it is not good enough to console oneself with the thought that the user was not supposed to behave in such ways!

There is a difficult issue raised by this sort of problem: how much responsibility lies with the programmer, and how much with the user? In *theory*, any problem specification agreed with a client for a program should specify exactly which user errors are the programmer's responsibility to deal with and which are the users' responsibility to avoid. In practice, the design and code is usually supposed to deal with the standard, predictable user errors without explicit specification. Nevertheless, this is a common area for disputes to arise between client and software producer!

In the first section of this unit some aspects of data validation and program testing will be considered. You must appreciate that there is much that could be done and said here. What *is* done is intended to make you aware of the problems and suggest, at a fairly elementary level, some of the many things that might be done.

Section 2 discusses various kinds of errors that arise in programming. Its purpose is to make you aware of some common error situations and, if possible, how to recover from them. During your work on this block you have probably made errors and been aware that, sometimes, Builder tries to diagnose what is wrong. The practical activities in this section demonstrate the presence of errors in programs, and provide an opportunity to investigate Builder's diagnostic messages.

The final section of the unit reviews most of what has been done in this block concerning problem solving. It should be just a quick read for you, but it is interspersed with revision exercises which might prove useful.

1 Validating and testing

Validation means many things when referring to software. Overall, it is the process of showing that a piece of software (a complete program or a module forming part of a program) performs to the specification laid down. In regard to data, it means ensuring that a data item meets the specification. In this section these ideas are dealt with at an elementary level, with **data validation** first.

1.1 Data validation

Computer programs invariably require input data on which they are to work. These data may be supplied via, for example, card readers, bar code readers, electronic disk or remote terminals. In an ideal world the input data provided would always be correct. In reality this does not occur, for card readers can misread (or fail to read) cards, and keyboard operators often hit wrong keys. As a result, a very large amount of computer software is written for the purpose of validating data associated with programs. Even in the context of the work in this block, where input has been confined to the keyboard, some validation of input has already been taking place, and more might have been considered in some of the designs.

In *Unit 2*, Sections 3 and 4, what seemed like a satisfactory solution to the 'mean' problem was reached. Here the user entered whole numbers in the (acceptable) range from 0 to 100 from the keyboard, or the sentinel value −1 to halt the loop. Now suppose for a moment that the user accidentally keys in 59 (or 588) when the intention was to enter 58. Having identified the error, the user would like to correct it. As it stands now, the design of the solution does not allow such correction to be made.

Validating user inputs can be built into the design. For example, the design could ensure that the integer that the user enters does lie in the range of admissible values (−1 to 100), by incorporating a **range check**. The steps which ask for and read in *NextNumber* might be replaced by a four-step loop such as the following.

1 **loop**
2   write out "Enter next number: "
3   read in *NextNumber*
4 **loopend when** (*NextNumber* ≥ −1) **and** (*NextNumber* ≤ 100)

(As this is not strictly a refinement of a single original step, it has not been numbered as such.)

This replacement will continue to loop, rejecting all integers outside the wanted range (without giving an error message in this case), moving on only when one in the correct range is received.

Unfortunately, knowing that the number read in is in the correct range gives no guarantee that the number is the one that the user intended, for it still might be the case that the number has been mistyped. Validation of this input could be taken a stage further by writing the entered number back to the screen and asking the user to confirm that the recorded number is the intended one. You will no doubt appreciate that by now the code for

Accidentally hitting a neighbouring key, or repeating one, are common keyboard errors, as is interchanging the order of two keypresses.

These steps were steps 3.1.1 and 3.1.2 of the design solution to the mean problem given in Subsection 3.2 of *Unit 2*.

validating this input would be getting quite complex. In any case, the program specification might not want every entry confirmed since that can be a time-consuming activity.

There is another issue pertinent to this. The design requires the user to enter integers lying in a certain range. But what will happen if the user keys in something which is not an integer? Suppose, for instance, that the value entered for *NextNumber* is 5o rather than 50, a mistake easily made and overlooked. The program will now be in all sorts of difficulty. How will the machine respond when, coded to read a whole number from the keyboard, it is given something that is not a whole number? You might have uncovered the answer to this question whilst carrying out the practical activities in *Units 2* and *3*, but if not (or you have forgotten), try the following experiment now.

Computer Activity 1.1

Start Builder and open a new console application. Save the project (File|Save Project As...) as B1U4ex11. Take the usual steps to make the library MT262io available for use and to hold the screen output. Use the Code Editor to add the following code just after the first opening brace.

Use the names B1U4ex11U and B1U4ex11.

```
int n;
  n = ReadIntPr("Enter number: ");
  WriteIntPr("The number entered was ", n);
```

Run the program several times entering each of the following strings in response to the prompt.

     23.78   − 23.78   23A   A23   23A37B   the null string (press Enter key)

What conclusions can you draw about the way *ReadIntPr* works?

Carry out a similar experiment to investigate how *ReadFloatPr* handles the input of strings which are of the wrong format to be of type **float**.

ReadInt works in just the same way but without the prompt for input.*

[*Solution on page 39*]

To use a computer effectively, two-way communication is essential. The user must be able to give information to the machine, telling it what to do and with what, and the machine has to pass back the results of its processing. The means by which humans and computers interact, referred to as the **user interface**, is a combination of software and hardware. The software controls the passage of data and specifies which hardware is to be involved.

Standard routines for reading data from keyboards and sending data to the monitor screen or printer, usually incorporating some data validation, exist in the user interfaces of systems. For the purposes of the programs of this block, the course team has provided some additional routines for you. The read and write functions in the library MT262io have been designed to customise existing C/C++ routines for your use. The intention was to provide functions that are easy to understand and use, accepting that they are somewhat limited in their capabilities. You might have felt, for instance, that *ReadIntPr* ought to reject entries such as 23A, but at least it does function as intended when the user does not do anything silly, and has enough built-in safeguards to avoid the program crashing when faced with input in the wrong format.

The interfaces seen by users of the programs you have written, provided by the console application template in Builder, are **command line user interfaces**. Here, instructions are via written commands which elicit specific responses from the computer. In Block III you will move on to write progams with **graphical user interfaces**. Here, manipulations of on-screen objects such as windows, icons, scroll bars, buttons and edit boxes are interpreted as commands to the computer. Builder provides a large library of software to support this interface. One feature of such interfaces is that they are supposedly 'friendlier' than command line interfaces, and this supposedly makes it more difficult for erroneous data to be entered. Nevertheless, you will see that data validation remains an issue.

The acronym GUIs, pronounced *goo-ease*, is in common use.

In *Unit 1* you were told that two-thirds of the software package that was used to typeset this course has the purpose of preventing and recovering from error situations. The example of the 'mean' problem might require a similar proportion of error-related code. While there was no great difficulty in reaching a solution to the problem as posed, to make it sufficiently robust to overcome all challenges that the keyboard operator might present requires a vast amount of supporting code. It can be quite a challenge to persuade a client to specify precisely which potential input errors should be handled by the software and which should be the responsibility of users.

Whilst recognising the presence of problems associated with the input of data, in the first two blocks of this course no great design and programming efforts will be made to overcome them. Such matters will be considered in greater depth when graphical user interface design is introduced in Block III.

1.2 Testing

In this block a number of problems have already been solved, and it was assumed each time that the method of solution (the algorithm) used was sound. This faith was no doubt increased by running the programs successfully using sample data. Before considering that a solution is complete, some systematic testing should be done to ensure that the solution does, indeed, function as specified. To that end, some sample data should be prepared — data against which the functioning of the program can be checked.

Consider again the 'mean' problem and assume that the range check to ensure all numbers entered do lie in the range from −1 to 100 has been incorporated. Under the assumption that the user, as requested, enters only integer data, what further testing is needed?

First, is the mean computed correctly when whole numbers in the correct range are entered? To test this, sample data is needed for which the mean can be calculated easily by hand. For example, the data set

$27, 31, 54, -1$

has a mean value (not counting the sentinel −1) of 37.33 to two decimal places. The program should produce this same answer. If it works correctly for three numbers, then it is probably going to work correctly for 4, 5, ... numbers in the correct range, so there is no need to repeat this test.

It is also important to ensure that the mean value is still worked out correctly when erroneous integer values have been input and rejected by the range check. The mean should still be 37.33 when the set

$$27, (111), 31, (222), (-54), 54, (-2), (101), -1$$

is entered, the numbers shown in brackets being excluded from the evaluation of the mean.

The sentinel value -1 plays a special role in the design. A start has been made above on checking that an entry of -1 is handled correctly; the first data set will test that as soon as an entry of -1 is made, the program calculates the mean and terminates. The checks have also ensured that the -1 sentinel value is not included in the calculation of the mean. There is one further possibility for problems associated with the sentinel value: what happens if -1 is the first entry made? Although that is not what is wanted (or sensible use of the program), the program does not preclude it. Indeed, the first entry is made in response to a prompt which asks for "the next number or -1 to stop". When -1 is entered as the first number, the loop terminates with no numbers having been counted towards the mean. The calculation of the mean goes on to divide zero by zero! You would be correct to anticipate that the machine is very unhappy about being asked to divide by zero! A flaw in the design has been discovered.

Exercise 1.1

How might the steps of the design given below be adapted to cater for -1 being keyed in as the first number, given that it is decided to assign the value zero to *Mean* if the value of *Count* is zero?

5.1.1 *Mean* $\leftarrow$ *Total*/*Count*
5.1.2 write out "The mean value is "
5.1.3 write out *Mean*

[*Solution on page 33*]

The course team design solution to the 'mean' problem is at the end of Subsection 3.2 of *Unit 2*.

The numbers 0 and 100 are also special in being the limits of the *acceptable* range of numbers for the design as modified by the discussion (in Subsection 1.1) of the input loop. Experience shows that such limits, sometimes called 'extreme values', should be included in test data. For instance, it is easy, in a big program, to fail to notice that you have the loop condition

1.1.1 **loop while** ... is less than ...

when what you really require is

1.1.1 **loop while** ... is less than or equal to ...

Testing with value 100 for *NextNumber* might well reveal such an error.

Overall, the following collection of data sets should be adequate to test the 'mean' program. (Of course, you can never be certain that you have covered all eventualities!)

Data set	Expected mean	Purpose of test
27, 31, 54, −1	37.33	Calculation of mean and −1 terminates input
27, 111, 31, 222, −54, 54, −1	37.33	Rejection of out-of-range entries
−1	00.00	Handling −1 as first entry
0, 0, 50, −1	16.67	Correct handling of 0
10, 50, 100, −1	53.33	Correct handling of 100

Exercise 1.2 _____

Look back at the solution of the Coin Tossing problem in the solution to Exercise 5.5 of *Unit 2*.

(a) What data validation might reasonably have been included in this solution?

(b) What happens if 'Q' is the first entry?

(c) Suggest a way of avoiding the problem with 'Q' as first entry.

(d) Suggest a set of data for testing the program.

(e) What flaw can you now see in the solution?

[*Solution on page 33*]

1.3 Trace tables

When should testing be carried out? If you are feeling really confident that a design is successful, there is a temptation to move straight on to the implementation stage. The program can be run and the sample data sets keyed in to check that the output is as expected. However, it is often advisable to test the program at design stage by carrying out a **hand trace**. That is, you imagine entering the selected sample data as you trace the steps of the design, keeping track of the values of all the variables as you go. If there are any flaws in the design, they will come to light as the values of the variables are discovered to behave in unexpected ways.

An example of a hand trace is given below.

As this course develops, you will see that a modular approach to program development is adopted. This means that large programs will always be broken into reasonably small chunks, for which the generic term is **modules**. The modules, which are subsequently combined to form the complete program, are independent, free-standing pieces of coded design which can be tested separately. It goes without saying that it is easier to locate errors in small modules than in large, whole programs; as a result, testing is confined to small bits of program.

Imagine that you have implemented a program which compiles successfully but when it runs it does not produce the expected results. Something has gone awry; there are **bugs** in your program, which therefore needs to be **debugged**. Almost always such bugs have been introduced at the design stage and are often quite well hidden. It may be that by running the program with sample data you can spot what is happening, and determine why it is happening, but it is recommended that, unless you can see quickly what has caused the problem, you do not experiment at your machine. It is better to go back to the drawing board and examine your design to test where its logic is failing. This could well involve a hand trace.

The idea of hand tracing a design is illustrated by looking at the solution to the Word Counting problem of *Unit 3*. For convenience, the design (from Subsection 4.2 of *Unit 3*) is reproduced below (with prompts omitted).

1.2   read in *Line*
2.1.1 *Index* ← 1
2.1.2 *Previous* ← '□'
2.1.3 *WordCount* ← 0
2.2.1 **loop while** *Index* ≤ *Length*(*Line*)
2.2.2   **if** (*Previous* = '□') **and** (*Line*[*Index*] ≠ '□') **then**
2.2.3   *WordCount* ← *WordCount* + 1
2.2.4   **ifend**
2.2.5   *Previous* ← *Line*[*Index*]
2.2.6   *Index* ← *Index* + 1
2.2.7 **loopend**
3.1   write out *WordCount*

In the **trace table** for this design, given below, there is one column for each of the variables *Index*, *WordCount* and *Previous*. In addition, a column is included for each of the conditions, namely the **loop** condition at step 2.2.1 and the compound **if** condition at step 2.2.2. Finally, as evaluation of the **if** condition refers to *Line*[*Index*], there is a column to record this value. The value of each condition at any time is either **true** or **false**, and this value determines which step follows in sequence. The column on the left of the trace table gives the step numbers in the sequence that are executed as the design is traced, but the **ifend** and **loopend** steps are omitted as they are just markers and contribute nothing as far as changing values is concerned.

The value of *Line* to be used is noted at the top of the table. As this does not change, it is not given a column.

The table traces the design for entry of the string "□Yes□", testing a single word with spaces at start and finish. A '?' entry in the table indicates that the variable concerned has not yet been assigned a value. Thereafter, whenever a step of the design changes the value of a variable, the revised value is recorded, so the current value of a variable at any time in the trace will be the last one listed in its column. The value of each condition is recorded each time that the step requiring its evaluation is reached.

Before actually doing the hand trace, it is important to have a clear idea of what *should* happen. The word count for this value of *Line* is 1, so the expectation is as follows.

o   *Index* should increase in steps of 1.
o   *Line*[*Index*] should proceed through the characters of "□Yes□" (and similarly for *Previous*).
o   *WordCount* should reach 1 after *Line*[*Index*] = 'Y' and should remain at that value.

The trace table follows.

Line is "□Yes□", Length(Line) is 5						
Condition 2.2.1: Index ≤ Length(Line)						
Condition 2.2.2: (Previous = '□') and (Line[Index] ≠ '□')						

Step	Index	WordCount	Previous	Condition 2.2.1	Line[Index]	Condition 2.2.2
2.1.1	1	?	?			
2.1.2			□			
2.1.3		0				
2.2.1				true		
2.2.2					□	false
2.2.5			□			
2.2.6	2					
2.2.1				true		
2.2.2					Y	true
2.2.3		1				
2.2.5			Y			
2.2.6	3					
2.2.1				true		
2.2.2					e	false
2.2.5			e			
2.2.6	4					
2.2.1				true		
2.2.2					s	false
2.2.5			s			
2.2.6	5					
2.2.1				true		
2.2.2					□	false
2.2.5			□			
2.2.6	6					
2.2.1				false		
3.1						

The trace table confirms that all is well for this example. The values of the variables change as predicted, the processing loop is exited after the final character, and the value of *WordCount* which will be written out in step 3.1, namely 1, is indeed correct.

Exercise 1.3

The data table and design given below are intended for a program that is concerned with sums of consecutive integers starting at 1, such as the sum of the first six integers:

$$1 + 2 + 3 + 4 + 5 + 6.$$

The purpose of the program is to determine how many integers have to be added in this way to make the sum exceed a target input by the user. For example, if the target is input as 30, then the required number would be 8 since $1 + 2 + 3 + 4 + 5 + 6 + 7 + 8$ exceeds 30 but the previous sum, with only 7 terms, does not.

Type	Identifier	Description
Integer	*Target*	The value to be exceeded, input by user
Integer	*Sum*	The (running) sum of the consecutive numbers
Integer	*Next*	The next integer which is added to the sum

1.1   write out "Enter target, which must be a positive integer: "

1.2   read in $Target$

2      $Sum \leftarrow 0$

3      $Next \leftarrow 1$

4   **loop while** $Sum \leq Target$

5         $Sum \leftarrow Sum + Next$

6         $Next \leftarrow Next + 1$

7   **loopend**

8   write out "Number of integers needed to exceed ", $Target$, " is ", $Next$

(a) Draw up a trace table for this design, assuming that 8 is entered at step 1 as the value of $Target$. Your table should include columns for the variables Sum and $Next$ and the condition in step 4, and should continue until the loop finishes execution. What is written out at step 8?

(b) Your trace should have revealed that there is a flaw in the design, since 4 numbers $(1 + 2 + 3 + 4)$ need to be added to exceed 8, but this is not the value that would be written out at step 8. Identify the cause of the problem and correct the design.

[Solution on page 34]

This section has introduced the location and correction of errors, using test data and trace tables as tools. In the next section, a classification of errors into various types is discussed, together with methods for tracking down the various types of error.

2 Debugging programs

Since designing a solution to a problem and then coding the design is a fairly involved process, it is reasonable to expect that errors will creep in at a number of points. These errors fall into several different categories, and different types of error are best tracked down by different methods.

This section is concerned with errors in the design and coding process. User errors are really a different problem; how they are dealt with should be part of the problem specification, as indicated in Section 1. It is possible to classify errors very crudely into **syntax errors** and **semantic errors**. Syntax is the structure of a design or program, without regard to what it does. For example,

> 'The abstract aeroplane swims in treacle.'

has the correct syntax (structure) for an English sentence. However, its semantics (meaning) is extremely dubious!

Correspondingly, it is quite possible to produce a design that uses all the words and phrases in the correct way, but whose meaning (the effect on input) is quite different from what was intended. It is even easier to make such errors when working in a language such as C++. Here, both types of error are investigated. For coded designs, Builder provides some useful facilities for tracking down both syntax and semantic errors.

Syntax is a noun but is often used as an adjective in place of the (correct) word 'syntactic'.

The course team has no wish to offend metaphysical poets, but it is quite hard to find a sentence that everyone would agree is total nonsense!

2.1 Syntax errors and semantic errors

If care is taken with a program design, the conversion to C++ code should be relatively straightforward. Nevertheless, you should not expect your coded programs to run successfully first time. Errors are readily made at all stages of the problem solving process, and they often do not come to light until the computer becomes involved.

Great care is needed, but this assertion is still true.

As indicated, errors divide into two main categories — syntax and semantic errors. As far as code is concerned, a syntax error is an error where the program does not conform to the rules of the programming language. Looked at another way, a syntax error has occurred whenever the compiler is unable to translate some intended statement of your program; you have written something that the compiler does not understand. Such errors often arise as typing errors as you enter your program from the keyboard. For example, an identifier might be misspelled or a semicolon or bracket might be missing. Of course, it might be more serious than a typing error; you might have misconstrued the syntax for coding one of your design steps. But syntax errors are, by and large, not difficult to detect because you will find that the compiler is very helpful. When a compilation fails, the compiler reports where, and why, it cannot compile what you have written. Just knowing the point of your program at which the compiler has experienced difficulty is often sufficient for you to spot what is wrong. The only time when the error is really hard to find is if the compiler cannot detect your error until it has read quite some way beyond it. For example, if you omit a semicolon, the compiler (usually) highlights the next statement, not the one lacking the semicolon. This is because the compiler did not know a semicolon was missing until it met something that had to have a semicolon preceding it.

Semantic errors are errors of the program logic. With a semantic error, the compiler is happy to translate the given C++ code into an executable program. However, when the program runs, one of two error situations may occur.

It is semantic errors which are referred to colloquially as **bugs**.

o   The program appears to run successfully, but not in the way the designer intended. Typically, the program yields results that are wrong.

o   The program fails to run successfully. It might 'crash' — halt during execution and report some error condition which prevents it continuing — or it might 'hang' — something causes it to go on and on forever, unable to complete its task.

By definition, the compiler cannot help you find semantic errors. The C++ code is 'grammatically' correct and has been translated. The instructions in the resulting executable program are carried out to the letter, and the system has no way of knowing that the designer really intended something else! So you are on your own in detecting and removing semantic errors — a process known as **debugging** your program. Sometimes the behaviour of the program at run-time steers you immediately to the cause of the semantic error. However, semantic errors are often deeply hidden, and debugging your program can be a difficult and time-consuming task.

Semantic errors can originate in a faulty design that is correctly translated into C++. Semantic errors can also be caused by such simple mistakes as placing a bracket or a semicolon in the wrong place during coding. (In both of these cases, the code may well be syntactically correct.) But more often they are flaws in the design logic and to debug a program you should refer back to your final design, which is free of C++ syntax concerns. (Designs have their own syntax rules.) The design style that you have been encouraged to adopt may help; the presence of **ifend**s and **loopend**s should highlight points where the various constructs terminate. If a visual inspection does not prove fruitful, you may need to carry out a trace to track down where things go wrong. As you will shortly see, Builder can help with the tracing process (as can most programming environments).

Ends of **if** and **loop** constructs are not immediately obvious in C++ code.

During your work in this block you will almost certainly have met some examples of syntax errors, and you might well have been confronted with semantic errors that the course team had not intended you to experience. If you feel you have already gained plenty of practice at recovering successfully from errors, you can omit the following computer activities, whose purpose is to let you witness some typical syntax and semantic error situations. To gain maximum benefit from Computer Activities 2.1–2.4, which are related, you should follow the instructions carefully and note all the points made in the solutions.

Computer Activity 2.1 _____

Start Builder and open the project ErrProg1.bpr. You will see an attempt to code the design of Exercise 1.3, with *Next* replaced by *Next* − 1 in step 8. (Somewhat briefer prompts have been used in the code.) Run the program. Note the messages that are displayed in the error window. Identify the two syntax errors which are being reported, but do *not* concern yourself with any other errors you might detect.

Use `Open Project...` from the `File` menu.

Computer Activity 2.2 _____

Correct the syntax errors discussed in the solution to Computer Activity 2.1, and run the program again. Try to explain the errors now being reported.

Computer Activity 2.3

Correct the syntax errors discussed in the solution to Computer Activity 2.2, and run the program again. It should now compile successfully. Test the program. Are you happy with the results the program is giving?

Computer Activity 2.4

In the Code Editor reverse the order of the two statements which are intended to form the **while** loop body to give the following (with the braces still missing).

```
Next = Next + 1;
Sum = Sum + Next;
```

Run the program and try to explain what happens. (You may need to read the solution to this activity to get out of difficulty.)

Computer Activity 2.5

Open the project `ErrProg2.bpr`. If you examine the code, you will see that the purpose of this program is to read in a string value from the keyboard and to write the first character to the screen.

(a) Run the program, and enter some string value to test the program.

(b) Run the program again, and enter the null string in response to the prompt. What happens? (You may need to read the solution to this activity to get out of difficulty.)

[*Solutions on page 39*]

2.2 Some common errors

Listed below are some of the more common syntax errors. The list is by no means complete, it is just a checklist of common mistakes to watch out for when coding your design into C++.

- o Typing errors and, in particular, misspelled identifiers. Remember that C++ is **case-sensitive**.
- o Using wrong symbols for operators. For example, it is all too easy to type '=' (instead of '==') when testing equality (because that does appear in designs as =).
- o Omitting variable declarations.
- o Missing round brackets (parentheses). In particular, remember that all conditions, whether part of an **if** statement or part of a **while** statement, must be enclosed in such brackets.
- o Misplaced or missing semicolons.
- o Misplaced or missing braces.

The compiler is very helpful in diagnosing the syntax errors that it uncovers. However, it is possible to get syntax wrong but still find that the compiler is quite happy with the program which has been presented. There was an example of this in Computer Activity 2.3, where a missing pair of braces did not cause a compilation error but resulted in something quite unexpected when the compiled program ran. It can happen in other ways. For example, typing '=' when the design logic requires '==' can result in code which reveals no syntax errors — the compiler can, in some circumstances, accept an assignment statement when the real intention was a test for equality.

The message is that you must not be complacent about syntax errors. The compiler will certainly help you find ones that it recognises. But syntax errors can manifest themselves as semantic errors, and errors which arise in this way are invariably difficult to detect.

The most difficult area of C++ syntax for beginners to master concerns the issues of where brackets, braces and semicolons are needed. In design, blocks of actions always have a marker at start and finish. For example, in an **if** step, **then** signals the start of the actions in the **then** branch and **else** or **ifend** signals the end of those actions. Since C++ has **else** but neither **then** nor **ifend**, quite a lot of care is needed in translating **if** statements correctly. Similar remarks apply to translating **loop** statements.

The indentation in a good design should highlight the various constructs. For example, if the design contains a **while** loop, then there will be a sequence of design steps starting at **loop** and finishing at **loopend** with the steps between indented. This whole loop represents (and codes as) a single statement in C++. The statement might, however, be a compound statement in that the body of the loop could itself be a sequence of two or more statements.

Consider the following design, in which *Index* is an integer variable and *Line* is a string variable. The steps have been numbered consecutively from 1 for reference purposes. (You need not worry about the purpose of the design.)

This is one area where C++ is an improvement on C. Early C compilers merely gave up when they found an error. To track down errors required a separate program called 'lint', so-called because it picked the fluff (lint) out of code!

```
1      read in Line
2      Count ← 0
3      Index ← 1
4      loop while Line[Index] ≠ '.'
5        if (Line[Index] ≥ 'A') and (Line[Index] ≤ 'Z') then
6          write out '*'
7          Count ← Count + 1
8        else
9          write out Line[Index]
10       ifend
11       Index ← Index + 1
12     loopend
13     write out Count
```

When this design is coded into C++ it will consist of 5 statements, namely a read in statement (step 1), followed by two assignment statements (steps 2 and 3), then a **while** statement (steps 4 to 12 inclusive), and finally a write out statement (step 13). The body of the **while** statement is a compound statement, itself consisting of a sequence of statements (corresponding to design steps 5 to 11 inclusive). The message is that any indented block of statements in a design is likely to translate to a block of C++ code enclosed in braces.

Exercise 2.1

Describe the C++ statements in the coding of the body of this **while** loop.

[*Solution on page 35*]

There are two important aspects of program syntax which this example illustrates. First, whenever a compound statement is involved, it is bound together by enclosing it in braces. So in the coding of the given design, the statements corresponding to steps 5 to 11 inclusive will need to be held in braces. Also, nested within this compound statement, the statements corresponding to steps 6 and 7 will have to be held in braces.

Second, when *individual* statements are coded, each requires an end-marker in the form of a semicolon. You can think of this semicolon as a separator marking the division between the statement to which it is appended and the next statement (if any). Individual statements need semicolons; the same is not true of compound statements. A compound statement will terminate in the semicolon of its last individual statement followed by the containing right brace; no additional separator is required.

The above remarks about moving from design to code are summarised in the 'design' given below. This 'design' is a copy of the previous design, but with the positions indicated where, when translated into C++ code, braces and semicolons will need to appear. The brackets which will be needed to hold the conditions in steps 4 and 5 are also shown. These brackets, braces and semicolons are **not** part of the design but are indicative of the sort of notes you might make for yourself to assist with the stage of converting from design to code.

There are already brackets round constituent parts of the condition in step 5. But the **if** syntax requires that the whole condition is held in brackets.

```
1    read in Line ;
2    Count ← 0 ;
3    Index ← 1 ;
4    loop while ( Line[Index] ≠ '.' )
     {
5      if ( (Line[Index] ≥ 'A') and (Line[Index] ≤ 'Z') ) then
       {
6        write out '*' ;
7        Count ← Count + 1 ;
       }
8      else
9        write out Line[Index] ;
10     ifend
11     Index ← Index + 1 ;
     }
12   loopend
13   write out Count ;
```

The **ifend** and **loopend** steps are very helpful markers in designs, but there is no directly associated coding for them.

Exercise 2.2 _____

Why are there no semicolons listed with either of steps 4 and 5?

Exercise 2.3 _____

Examine the design given below, which involves two integer variables *Next* and *Target*. Decide where brackets, braces and semicolons are going to be needed when this design is coded.

```
1    read in Target
2    if Target % 2 = 1 then
3      Next ← Target
4      loop
5        Next ← 3 * Next − 1
6        loop
7          Next ← Next/2
8        loopend when Next % 2 = 1
9        write out Next
10     loopend when Next ≤ Target
11   ifend
```

[*Solutions on page 35*]

_____

You may now appreciate why you have been encouraged to make use of indentation in your designs, and to indent the corresponding C⁺⁺ code carefully. You may also now appreciate why the course team uses the coding convention in which an opening brace is vertically aligned with the corresponding closing one.

There are other conventions adopted in certain software companies, but this one is fairly widely used.

2.3 Walking through a program

Tracing a design by hand can prove to be a most effective way of rooting out semantic errors. However, as you may well have sensed from the examples seen, it can also be a time-consuming activity. Fortunately, most implementations of programming languages these days provide features to help with tracing a program once it has been coded and is running (though not necessarily in the required way). Builder is no exception, in that it offers facilities for **walking through a program**; that is, rather than running the program at its normal speed, it can be executed in steps in ways that allow the user to inspect what is going on.

Sometimes this procedure is called **stepping** through a program.

To complete this section on errors you are going to use Builder's help to walk through the solution reached for the Calculator Simulation problem of *Unit 3*, Section 2. As you walk through the program, you will witness something very similar to the design trace table. With Builder doing the bulk of the work, you will be able to watch how the variables and conditions in the program change value as statements are executed. The remainder of this section is presented as one on-going practical activity. Your task will be to follow the fifteen bulleted instructions. There are no solutions to the parts of this activity; instead, commentary is given between the instructions. Please read each instruction right through before carrying it out.

o   Start Builder and open the project `CTCalc.bpr`. Now you should be looking at the Code Editor window displaying the course team version of the program.

The first task is to draw up a list of the expressions (variables and conditions) whose values it is useful to inspect as the program is running. These expressions form the **Watch List** and are essentially the expressions which would have been chosen as column headings if you were to hand trace the design of this program. There are three variables used in the program, namely *Answer*, *NextVal* and *Operator*, and two conditions, one controlling the post-conditioned **do while** statement and one controlling the **if** statement which avoids division by zero. These five items will make up the Watch List.

o   In the Code Editor window, left click anywhere inside *any* occurrence of the variable *Answer*. Right-click the mouse button. In the popup menu that appears, choose `Debug|Add Watch at Cursor`. The Watch List window opens with the following single item listed.

Ctrl+F5 is a shortcut for this process.

Answer:[process not accessible]

This just indicates that no value exists for the expression *Answer* at present.

(If no expression is at the cursor when you right-click the mouse button, the popup menu referred to above appears. But if you now select `Debug|Add Watch at Cursor`, a new dialog box, entitled `Watch Properties`, appears. You can now type `Answer` in the Expression box. Having made sure that the only item selected (of the nine) is `Default`, click on `OK`. This method is more time-consuming than the one above.)

In what follows, you need to view the Code Editor window and the Watch List window simultaneously. To help with this, right-click in the `Watch List` window, and select `Stay on Top` from the popup menu.

o   Click in the Code Editor window, and add the variables *NextVal* and *Operator* to the Watch List by doing exactly the same as you did for *Answer*.

If you 'lose' the Watch List window, you can recover it by choosing `Debug Windows|Watches` from the `View` menu.

To add a condition to the Watch List, it is necessary to highlight the whole of the condition before right-clicking the mouse button.

o   Highlight the whole of the condition

```
Operator != '='
```

in the Code Editor window, right-click the mouse button, and choose `Debug|Add Watch at Cursor` to add this condition to the Watch List.

Repeat these actions for the condition

```
NextVal != 0
```

You have now added all the required items to the Watch List, but there is one final task before running the program.

o   In the Code Editor window, left-click anywhere in the line

```
switch (Operator)
```

near the middle of the code. Right-click the mouse button to reveal the pull-down menu. This time click on `Debug|Toggle Breakpoint`. The chosen line of code becomes highlighted in red. (Here and below it is assumed that you have not altered Builder's default colour settings.) In the left-hand margin next to the line, the breakpoint icon appears — a red circle.

This line of code will be permanently highlighted until the breakpoint is removed by using `Debug|Toggle Breakpoint` again.

The purpose of a **breakpoint** is to pause execution of a running program there. At a breakpoint the user can inspect the progress of a program by means of, for example, a Watch List (which displays the current values of chosen expressions). Execution has then to be restarted manually from the breakpoint Any number of breakpoints may be included in a program, and if, for example, a breakpoint is placed inside a loop body, then it may be encountered many times and each time execution will pause there.

There are other progress inspection features not introduced here.

What you have done has placed just one breakpoint *inside* the main loop of the program. When the program is run, it will proceed as normal until it reaches the breakpoint for the first time. Then, as you will see, there are a number of ways in which you can proceed.

o   Select `Run|Run` to run the program.

Alternatively, click on the green triangle speed button or press `F9`.

The familiar program window will open with the prompt for you to enter the first number. (Do *not* do this yet.) Also the Code Editor and Watch List windows will disappear at this point, but will have reappeared when you next need them.

As the program runs, you are going to need to see the Code Editor window and the Watch List window in addition to the program one. As long as some of each window is visible, you will be able to switch between them as necessary, by clicking. (You may need to move the Code Editor window or the program window to ensure that neither window fully obscures the other.)

o   Enter 23 in response to the prompt, and watch what happens as you press `Enter`.

The Code Editor and Watch List windows open. In the Watch List the current values of the three variables are now listed. What is more, the two conditions are each shown as having value **true**, which is consistent with the variable values. The Code Editor window looks much as you last saw it, with the breakpoint highlighted. There are, however, two changes on the left of the window. The extreme left-hand end of the breakpoint step has acquired a new marker (a green tick over the red circle and a green arrow), which will be explained in a moment. Also there is a series of blue dots to indicate the executable steps in the code

o Select Run|Run to restart the run of the program. Enter '−' in response to the prompt for the next operator, and 11 in response to the prompt for the next number. Note that the program now runs until it meets the breakpoint again. Observe the values now in the Watch List window.

By running the program right through in this way, you have a means of checking the values of variables at each pass through the main loop. It is also possible to take things even more slowly.

o Press the F8 key, and try to explain what happens in the Code Editor window.

It is possible to execute a program using the Step Over facility, by which execution can be made to happen one step at a time. Pressing the F8 key causes the next step to be executed. The **switch** step at the breakpoint has just been executed and a new highlight shows the next step to be executed. In addition to this highlight, the next step is indicated by a green arrow marker at its extreme left-hand end. The marker is at

```
case '-' : Answer = Answer - NextVal;
```

which is the correct selection from the case list, since the current value of *Operator* is '−'. If F8 is pressed again, this line of code will be executed.

o Press F8 and note what happens, checking the resulting changes to the Watch List.

The green arrow moves to the **break;** statement immediately after the step just executed.

o Press F8 again.

o Press F8 again. This executes the step which reads in the next operator. To complete this step, you must first click in the *program* window to enable you to respond to the prompt. Enter '/' and note what happens when the Enter key is pressed.

The Code Editor window should now have

```
while (Operator != '=');
```

highlighted, and this will be executed when F8 is next pressed. The Watch List confirms that the current value of this condition is **true**, so the loop will be iterated again.

o Press F8 twice, and enter 0 in response to the prompt for the next number (remembering to first click in the program window so that the number can be entered). Press F8 five more times to trace the program through the code which avoids division by zero.

You should now explore these facilities further, at your leisure. You can mix running to the next breakpoint (by selecting Run|Run) with progressing one step at a time (pressing F8).

The Step Over facility is on the Run menu. The keyboard equivalent is F8.

This green arrow marker was noted when the breakpoint step was the next step to be executed.

If you see
[process not accessible]
in the Watch List, ignore it.

When you are ready to stop, do the following.

o Wherever you are in the program, run it. When the request in the program window for an operator is reached, enter '='. The program will now run normally to its completion, as the breakpoint is not encountered again. Before closing the project, right-click on the line at which the breakpoint was set and select Debug|Toggle Breakpoint from the popup menu to remove the breakpoint, and then close the Watch List window.

In pursuing this example there was no specific objective other than to let you sample some of the facilities that Builder offers. You will have seen the value of being able to trace the progress of a program by walking through it in this way.

3 Review of the problem solving process

As was stated in *Units 2* and *3*, there are no hard and fast rules for how to go about problem solving. Some general guidelines were given, and you gained some experience of ways of attacking aspects of the problem solving process. There are five main stages in the process, as follows.

1. Understand the problem.
2. Design a solution.
3. Implement the solution.
4. Test the solution.
5. Document the solution.

Problem solving is a creative process, not merely a linear progression through the steps of each of the stages. Rather, the solver goes back and repeats steps, several times if necessary, until satisfied with the solution. Here, each of the main stages is summarised, with the key ideas on design and coding encountered in the block being revisited.

3.1 Understand the problem

The necessity to understand the posed problem must seem obvious. However, the specification of a problem often requires clarification and further information, and you, the solver, should be prepared to ask enough questions, and uncover enough detail, to discover precisely what it is that you are expected to do. Even in the small designs tackled in this block, ambiguities were recognised and decisions taken on just which version of a problem to tackle. At a deeper level, suppose you are asked to write a computer program whose purpose is to bring up to date a bank's daily account balances. To clarify this task, there is much more information that you need, and you may well ask the following questions, amongst others.

○ What kinds of account are involved? Cheque? Deposit? Both?

○ How many accounts are involved? A few hundred? Many thousands?

○ Is the solution to deal with both deposits and withdrawals?

○ What should be done if an account becomes overdrawn?

○ In what form will the information be received? On paper, disk, or what?

○ Is there a time limit to be considered, i.e. must the updating process be completed by a certain time of day?

Once the problem is understood as fully as possible, you can turn to the task of effecting a solution. It may well be that you decide not to launch yourself into solving the most general form of the problem. As you saw with the Word Counting problem, it is sometimes advisable to solve simpler, special cases of the problem first, with the intention of adapting and extending the simpler solution to cater for the general form of the problem.

3.2 Design a solution

The ultimate goal is to reach a solution to a problem which can be implemented on a computer. This condition is very restrictive because, as you will already have started to appreciate, a computer is capable of performing only a limited number of simple tasks, albeit extremely quickly. The solution is first developed in the form of a design. Reaching a design solution is the creative, and invariably the most difficult, phase of the problem solving process. (Your skill at design will increase during the course, with further practice.)

The top-down approach to design, and the design conventions introduced in this block, are not standard, but one objective in this course is to keep the design solution machine-independent. This means that a successful design should be expressed in terms of basic machine operations and should be capable of being implemented on any machine, using any programming language. (This is a little ambitious: 'most' machines and 'most' languages is a more reasonable aim.) In this course, the language C++ is used for practical work, but the design conventions are not exclusive to C++.

Any consistent, methodical approach to problem solving will have similar features.

The top-down methodology involves starting with a solution in very broad terms. The first attempt at a solution, the top-level design, should focus on key aspects of what is going to be involved, leaving aside all detail. Two prototypes have been suggested for top-level designs. For many programs the overall plan involves inputting data, then processing the data, and finally outputting the results of the processing. For such programs, the following three-step top-level design captures this plan.

1   read in the data
2   process the data
3   write out results

However, there are many situations where a more natural solution will have the input and process phases merging, so that some data are being processed before other data are entered. The above prototype could be modified to the following two-step top-level design.

1   input and process data
2   write out results

For such solutions, the top-level design might incorporate just a little detail to the input and process phase by recognising the need for iteration in the solution, as follows.

1   initialise variables
2   **loop while** there are more data items to be processed
3   read in and process next data item
4   **loopend**
5   write out results

From the top-level design, you grapple with each aspect of the broad solution, gradually and systematically filling in more detail as the steps are refined. This approach encourages the breaking up of problems into subtasks which can be handled separately. For example, in the first of the top-level designs mentioned above, the three tasks of reading in data, processing data and writing out results can be treated as individual design problems, although they will be involved with common data. Each of these subtasks might itself break up into a number of smaller subtasks to be carried out in some sequence.

The first stage in progressing from the top-level design towards refinement must be to give thought to the data in the problem. The program has to store, manipulate and retrieve values of the data with which it is to work. This is achieved through the use of variables, each of which has an identifier. Thinking about what variables your design is going to use, and what type they need to be, is an important step in the design process. The first attempt at a data table will usually require modification during refinement: the need for additional variables may be uncovered, or an original variable may not be required.

A variable is an area of the computer's memory, used for holding a data item.

Exercise 3.1

What five types of variable have been encountered in this block?

[Solution on page 36]

In designing solutions to problems, you are limited to a number of features, and constructs, with which the computer can cope. The solution is described in terms of a sequence of steps, each step being something which can be coded into an unambiguous instruction for the computer to carry out. The steps are executed in sequence as listed, except when branching and iteration are involved. You may feel that you have been exposed to quite a lot of design constructs in this block, but the reality is that there are very few. The principal design problem is to use the limited number of constructs correctly to effect the solution.

The design constructs which you have met in this block will now be reviewed. They are:
o   the assignment step,
o   the read in step,
o   the write out step,
o   the if step,
o   the case step,
o   the while loop,
o   the when loop.

The assignment step is used more than any other. It takes the simple form

Variable ← Value

Here *Variable* is the identifier for some variable.

and its versatility comes from the wide range of ways in which the value on the right-hand side can arise — a constant value, the current value of some variable, an expression involving variables and operations. In all cases, the value must be compatible with the type of the variable on the left. For example, if the left-hand side is the identifier of a real variable, then any expression assigned to it must evaluate to a real number. The expression may well involve other variables, together with various operations which are appropriate for the data types involved.

The course team has consciously kept the 'read in' and 'write out' steps very simple at design level. As you will no doubt appreciate by now, the implementation of these steps does require a little thought and care, for it depends on the types of the data being read or written. The read in step is a variant of the assignment statement; it assigns a value to a variable, but the value is read from the keyboard rather than being the value of an expression. It takes the following form.

  read in *Variable*

When a program requires keyboard input, it should issue a prompt. This is one role for the write out step. The write out step is used to write messages to the screen, to write the values of variables to the screen, or a combination of the two. It takes the form

  write out "This is a message ", *Variable*

where either the string message, or the variable, can be omitted.

The **if** step is the principal way of introducing branching into a design. It takes the following form.

  if condition **then**
    steps of **then** branch
  else
    steps of **else** branch
  ifend

The **then** and **else** branches might themselves be quite complex designs, possibly involving further branching.

The space before the closing double quote is not essential here, but is in preparation for coding that will make the screen output readable.

Unit 2, Subsection 3.2

Exercise 3.2

Some examination marks, which are whole numbers in the range 0 to 100, are converted to grades as follows.

  Grade A   80 and over
  Grade B   66 to 79
  Grade C   40 to 65
  Grade D   0 to 39

Design an **if** step whose purpose is to write out the grade corresponding to a mark. (The solution uses the character variable *Grade* and the integer variable *Mark*.)

[*Solution on page 36*]

The solution to Exercise 3.2 gives a clue as to how complex an **if** step would become if a large number of different cases had to be dealt with. A neater way of branching into three or more paths is provided by the **case** step, which takes the following form.

  select case depending on value of expression
    value 1 : actions appropriate to value 1
    value 2 : actions appropriate to value 2
      ⋮
    value *n* : actions appropriate to value *n*
  else
    default action
  selectend

Unit 3, Subsection 1.2

Each of value 1, value 2, ..., value *n* must be the same type as the expression in the **select case** step evaluates to.

Exercise 3.3 ————————————————————

A filling station sells diesel fuel at 78.9p per litre, unleaded petrol at 77.9p per litre, regular petrol at 79.9p per litre and super petrol at 82.9p per litre. Write a design whose purpose is to receive, from the keyboard, a real value *NumberOfLitres* and a character value *Type* where 'D' stands for diesel, 'U' for unleaded, 'R' for regular and 'S' for super, and to write out the cost of purchasing this number of litres of this type of fuel.

These figures were not untypical for mid-2001.

[*Solution on page 37*]

In this block you have worked with two loop constructs. The pre-conditioned **while** loop takes the form

> **loop while** condition
>   steps of loop body
> **loopend**

Unit 3, Subsection 1.3

and the post-conditioned **when** loop takes the form

> **loop**
>   steps of loop body
> **loopend when** condition

In each case, the condition can be any expression, no matter how complex, which gives a boolean value. The loop body consists of any number of design steps, possibly including other loops, which are executed repeatedly until the controlling condition becomes **false** (**while** loop) or **true** (**when** loop). In the next block you will meet and use another loop construct, the unconditioned **for** loop.

It is actually possible to design any loop requirement using only suitably constructed **while** loops. (You are not expected to find this statement 'obvious'.) In practice, **while** and **for** loops are widely used, but **when** loops are probably rather under-used.

Exercise 3.4 ————————————————————

Write a design whose purpose is to read in a non-empty string from the keyboard and to write out the string to the screen backwards. For example, the input of "STAR" would be written out as "RATS". (You will find it helpful to make use of the *Length* function. The final character of a non-empty string *MyStr* is at index *Length*(*MyStr*).)

[*Solution on page 37*]

What may come as a pleasant surprise to you is to learn that the list of design steps just summarised is, to all intents and purposes, a complete list. The three loops and two branching processes are all that are needed. You will meet many further types of data, with supported operations, so that assignment statements can be more complex. The read in and write out steps will have to be more versatile to cater for more types and allow, for example, reading from disk (instead of keyboard) and writing to a printer (instead of the screen). But there are no further basic design constructs to be met.

In these early stages of development, when faced with a programming problem you will have to design your solution from scratch. However, as experience grows you should, when confronted with a problem, ask yourself: does this remind me of some other problem that I have met in the past? You can often gain invaluable clues from previously solved problems to help you with solving new ones. Indeed, before too long, re-using existing software to help solve new problems will become a vital technique.

When the design solution is finished, it is sound advice to test it before moving on to implementation. Semantic errors are, by and large, made at the design stage and tend to be easier to spot while design matters are fresh in the mind, and designs ought to be more comprehensible than their coded version. However, it is quite often the case that attempts to implement the design have taken place before errors come to light and, as you have seen, the machine can be used in a helpful way to track down errors.

3.3 Implement the solution

At the implementation stage, the design is coded into the chosen programming language and implemented on the machine. If care and effort have been put into the design stage, then implementation should be straightforward. If unexpected error situations occur, then the programmer should return to the design stage rather than try to 'hack' the code to make the program work!

The coding of a design requires translation of each of the design steps into the corresponding statement in the chosen programming language (here C++), declaring all variables, and putting the individual parts together to form the overall program. Once you understand the syntax of the individual statements, you are well on your way to mastering the coding challenge.

There is one further complication. At design level, the catch-all phrases *read in* and *write out* are used for the input from the keyboard and output to the monitor screen. At implementation, different routines are required to handle different types of data; for example, you cannot use the routine that reads in a real number to read in a string value. Whenever a design involves a read or write step, you will need to think carefully about which of the available functions to use.

The following three exercises are intended to revise coding of some of the main design steps. They offer ample opportunity to revise how to use the read and write functions.

You may need to refer to *Units 2* and *3* or the Handbook for any coding details which escape you.

Exercise 3.5 ————————————

Write a fragment of code for the design of Exercise 3.2, including the variable declarations. (Assume that the value of *Mark* has been read in.)

Exercise 3.6 ————————————

Write a fragment of code for the design of Exercise 3.3, including the variable declarations.

Exercise 3.7 ————————————

Write a fragment of code for the design of Exercise 3.4, including the variable declarations.

[*Solutions on page 37*]

3.4 Test the solution

When your coded solution is fully implemented, the results that it gives must be tested. You should look back at the problem specification to make sure that what you have achieved really does solve the problem as posed (and clarified). During the design stage, you may have been borrowing ideas from a solution to an earlier problem, or solving a simpler case of the problem first, and it is all too easy to lose track of the real objective.

Even when you believe that you have solved the posed problem, careful testing that the program functions correctly is needed. It is not uncommon for a computer program to work most of the time, whilst being caught out by extreme conditions. For example, a program to search a list of data items might always work successfully except when the item required is the last item in the list. The designer might have overlooked the fact that different conditions pertain when the search ends successfully at the very end of the list. It may be a long time before the program is run with the last item being the one sought, and hence a long time before it comes to light that the solution is flawed.

The designer should consider that part of the task is to draw up a list of test data—data to test the correct functioning of the program. This should involve thinking about the extreme cases which need to be handled by the program. For example, for a program that counted the number of words in a line of text given by the user, the extreme conditions to be tested would include input of an empty line, input of a line with space characters and nothing else, and input of a line with no space characters. Any one of these could cause the coded program to crash if the solution has not catered for such an input.

The program developed in *Unit 3* did cater for such inputs. See Computer Activity 4.1 of that unit.

3.5 Document the solution

Throughout the solution process it is important that a written record is kept of what has been done. The solution to a problem cannot consist of a C++ program in isolation; it must be supported by other documentation. For a small task like the 'mean' problem, at present you know what it does and how to use it. Will you remember in 12 months' time if you come across the program again unexpectedly? What if you are asked to modify the program, to take into account some minor change in the specification? Some way is needed of recalling just what design decisions were taken, and why. Relying on the ability to recall all the details just by reading the listing of the program code is unlikely to be sufficient. (One of the inventors of the C language described it as 'write only', implying that C code was more or less unreadable! With care, C++ code need not be this bad, but supporting documentation will always help.)

Other documentation divides into two types: **user documentation** and **programmer documentation**. The user documentation is intended for the user of the program, explaining all features of the software and how to use it. Remember that it is usually going to be others, not the designer, who will use the program. If you have ever used a word-processor, for example, you will appreciate the need for a user manual to guide you in using the software successfully. The programmer documentation contains technical details of the program, and is aimed at giving a full appreciation of the design and implementation of the program to anyone (including the designer) who may want to modify the program.

For the relatively small projects with which you are to be concerned in the early part of this course, you need not be too concerned with *formal* documentation of the design; the development of the top-level design and its refinements are usually sufficient. You are, however, advised to make your own notes on aspects of each program that you write. There is one useful device which the course team has been using. In designs and C++ programs, explanatory comments can be included. In C++, comments are preceded by the double forward slash, //. On any line in the listing of the program code, everything which follows // is a comment and is non-executable. You will have witnessed examples of such lines in MT262 program templates and Builder's own program templates. You are expected to make use of comments in your programs.

It is possible to put longer comments in C++ by surrounding them with /* ... */. However, short one-line comments, to the point, are encouraged.

The same convention is adopted in designs; anything following // on a line in a design is a comment. Comments in designs will often be given a whole line to themselves, in which case the line will not be given a step number. The main purpose of a comment in a design is to help readers understand various features of the design. For example, in the solution to the Word Counting problem, the start of a word was recognised by finding a space character followed by a non-space. A casual reader of the design might find this aspect of the design difficult to comprehend, but a comment in the design would help. The whole design might be annotated as follows. Remember that the data table, which is a crucial part of the design documentation but which is not included here, will explain the roles of the variables.

// Count the number of words in a given line of text

1.1   write out "Enter a non-empty line of text: "

1.2   read in *Line*

2.1.1 *Index* ← 1
      // Previous set to '□' to recognise word starting at index 1

2.1.2 *Previous* ← '□'

2.1.3 *WordCount* ← 0

2.2.1 **loop while** *Index* ≤ *Length*(*Line*)
      // Recognise start of word by space followed by non-space

2.2.2   **if** (*Previous* = '□') **and** (*Line*[*Index*] ≠ '□') **then**

2.2.3   *WordCount* ← *WordCount* + 1

2.2.4   **ifend**

2.2.5   *Previous* ← *Line*[*Index*]

2.2.6   *Index* ← *Index* + 1

2.2.7 **loopend**

3.1   write out "Number of words in text is ", *WordCount*

The same set of comments could be added to the coding of this design. In template programs which are provided from time to time, and for which no design is offered, you will often find that comments have been added for your benefit in this way.

Exercise 3.8 _____

In Subsection 2.1 of *Unit* 3 there is a final design for the Calculator
Simulation problem. What comments might have been added to that
design to help you (or another casual reader) understand the design?

[*Solution on page 38*]

Objectives

After studying this unit, you should be able to:

o   draw up suitable data sets to test a program;

o   trace a design by hand using a trace table;

o   make use of trace tables to detect errors;

o   interpret and act on error messages appearing in Builder's Code Editor
    window;

o   use the Watch List facility, breakpoints and the `Step Over` facility
    (with guidance) to walk through a program;

o   add comments to designs and code as a form of solution documentation;

o   use and understand the use of the following terms: data validation,
    range check, user interface, hand trace, trace table, module,
    semantic error, syntax error, walking (or stepping) through a program.

Solutions to the Exercises

Section 1

Solution 1.1

As the design stands, the calculation of *Mean* involves division of *Total* by *Count*. So it is necessary to make sure that *Count* is not zero at this time. Given the decision to assign the value zero to *Mean* if the value of *Count* is zero, it is sufficient to refine only step 5.1.1, as below. (The numbering is of the refinement only, for brevity.)

```
1    if Count ≠ 0 then
2        Mean ← Total/Count
3    else
4        Mean ← 0
5    ifend
```

Thus step 5.1.3

write out *Mean*

can result in 0 being written out only if each number entered is a zero, or −1 is the first entry.

Solution 1.2

(a) The user has to enter one of three permitted characters, namely 'H', 'T' or 'Q'. The program does not cater for any other entry by the user. In fact, the entry of any spurious character would result in both *Total* and *SeqCount* being erroneously incremented. You might reasonably include a check that the user entry is one of three admissible characters by, for instance, replacing the step

3.1.2 read in *Toss*

by the following loop refinement.

```
1    loop
2        read in Toss
3    loopend when Toss is equal to one of 'H', 'T' or 'Q'
```

This loop will be exited only when one of the three admissible characters is entered. As a result, no inadmissible entry is processed in later steps; that is, the program ignores inadmissible entries.

An alternative, making use of ideas from *Unit 3*, is to use a **select case** step (together with the C++ **switch** implementation) which has cases for the three permissible values and ignores all others.

(b) A first entry of 'Q' will cause the loop to exit immediately. The result is that division by zero will be attempted when the calculation of the mean is done.

(c) A possible fix is to test *SeqCount* for being zero before attempting to calculate the mean, just as in the solution to Exercise 1.1.

(d) The need is to check that the mean is calculated correctly, that inadmissible characters are simply ignored in the calculations and that entry of 'Q' terminates the program. In addition, extreme conditions should be considered. At least there should be a check that all is well when at most one of 'H' or 'T' is included in the data, either alone or several times. The following table gives a suitable collection of data sets. (The 'X', 'Y' and 'Z' in the table can be replaced by any characters other than 'H', 'T' and 'Q'. In particular, note that the expected mean for the second data set may be obtained by imagining that each 'X' is not present, which is equivalent to it being ignored by the program, and calculating the mean in the normal way.)

Data set	Expected mean	Purpose of test
HHTTTHHTTTTQ	2.75	Calculation of mean and Q terminates the program
HHXTTTXXHHXTTXTQ	2.50	Ignoring inadmissible entries
Q	?	Handling Q as first entry
XYZQ	?	Handling no H or T entered
XHXXHQ	2.0	Handling no T entered
HHQ	2.0	Handling only Hs entered
TQ	1.0	Handling T alone entered

(e) The '?'s in the above table pinpoint problems that thinking about extreme conditions has brought to light. The problem specification should inform us what to do if the input does not include either an 'H' or a 'T' (notwithstanding the fact that the program would be somewhat pointless). Should the solution report that "No data was entered." or that the mean length of no sequences of equal outcomes is zero? The design as it stands has ignored this eventuality and, should it arise, goes on to calculate a mean value!

Solution 1.3

(a) A trace table is as follows.

Target is 8, Condition 4: Sum ≤ Target			
Step	Sum	Next	Condition 4
2	0	?	
3		1	
4			true
5	1		
6		2	
4			true
5	3		
6		3	
4			true
5	6		
6		4	
4			true
5	10		
6		5	
4			false
8			

Step 8 writes out

> Number of integers needed to exceed 8 is 5.

(b) The design appears to be functioning correctly. *Next* increases by 1
each time and *Sum* has the right sequence of values. However, the
wrong value is written out at step 8. The problem is that the design
keeps the variable *Next* one ahead of the count of how many numbers
have been added so far. Hence it is *Next* − 1 which should be written
out, and the simple way of putting the design right is to replace *Next*
by *Next* − 1 in step 8.

With this proposed correction, the design remains open to the criticism
that the variable *Next* is being misused. It has two purposes in the
program:

o   it keeps track of the next number to be added to the sum;

o   it is used as the count of how many numbers have been added.

The error situation came about because these two values differ by 1.
There are neater ways of amending this design so that *Next* has a
single purpose in the program, but they will not be discussed here.

Section 2

Solution 2.1
The body of the **while** loop comprises two statements: an **if** statement
(steps 5 to 10) followed by an assignment statement (step 11). The **if**
statement has the feature that its **then** clause involves two statements and
so is a compound statement.

Solution 2.2
The syntax of the **while** loop in C++ is

```
while (condition)
{single or compound statement}   //Braces are not essential if single statement.
```

and the syntax of the **if** statement is

```
if (condition)
{single or compound statement}
else   // else part is optional if action is 'do nothing'.
{single or compound statement}
```

In neither case is there a semicolon following the condition. (Note the use
of comments in the above code fragments.)

Solution 2.3

The **then** clause (steps 3 to 10) and the body of the outer loop (steps 5 to 9) are each compound statements, and so must have holding braces. The inner loop has just a single statement (step 7) in its body, so the braces are not necessary. Each of the three conditions needs to be held in brackets.

It is not an error to have braces holding a single statement.

```
1     read in Target ;
2     if ( Target % 2 = 1 ) then
      {
3        Next ← Target ;
4        loop
         {
5           Next ← 3 * Next − 1 ;
6           loop
7              Next ← Next/2 ;
8           loopend when ( Next % 2 = 1 ) ;
9           write out Next ;
         }
10       loopend when ( Next ≤ Target ) ;
      }
11    ifend
```

Section 3

Solution 3.1

Integer, real, character, string and boolean.

Solution 3.2

One suitable design is as follows.

```
1       if Mark ≥ 80 then
2          Grade ← 'A'
3       else
4.1        if Mark ≥ 66 then
4.2           Grade ← 'B'
4.3        else
4.4.1         if Mark ≥ 40 then
4.4.2            Grade ← 'C'
4.4.3         else
4.4.4            Grade ← 'D'
4.4.5         ifend
4.5        ifend
5       ifend
6       write out "Grade is ", Grade
```

Solution 3.3

The course team design makes use of a real variable *Cost*.

1.1 write out "Enter number of litres: "
1.2 read in *NumberOfLitres*
2.1 write out "Enter fuel type: "
2.2 read in *Type*
3   **select case** depending on *Type*
4.1   'D' : *Cost* ← *NumberOfLitres* * 78.9
4.2   'U' : *Cost* ← *NumberOfLitres* * 77.9
4.3   'R' : *Cost* ← *NumberOfLitres* * 79.9
4.4   'S' : *Cost* ← *NumberOfLitres* * 82.9
5   **else**
6   write out "Type not recognised. Please re-enter transaction."
7   **selectend**
8   write out "The cost in pence is ", *Cost*

Solution 3.4

This solution uses *MyStr* as the string variable whose value is to be read in and reversed. The objective is to write out in order the characters at indexes

$Length(MyStr), Length(MyStr) - 1, Length(MyStr) - 2, \ldots, 2, 1$

of *MyStr*. For this purpose, an integer variable *Index* is used for access to the characters.

1   read in *MyStr*
2   *Index* ← *Length(MyStr)*
3   **loop while** *Index* ≥ 1
4   write out *MyStr*[*Index*]
5   *Index* ← *Index* − 1
6   **loopend**

Solution 3.5

```
int Mark;
char Grade;
 if (Mark >= 80)
   Grade = 'A';
 else
   if (Mark >= 66)
     Grade = 'B';
   else
     if (Mark >= 40)
       Grade = 'C';
     else
       Grade = 'D';
  WriteCharPr("Grade is ", Grade);
```

Solution 3.6

```
float NumberOfLitres;
float Cost;
char Type;
 NumberOfLitres = ReadFloatPrCr("Enter number of litres: ");
 Type = ReadCharPrCr("Enter fuel type: ");
 switch (Type)
 {
   case 'D' : Cost = NumberOfLitres * 78.9; break;
   case 'U' : Cost = NumberOfLitres * 77.9; break;
   case 'R' : Cost = NumberOfLitres * 79.9; break;
   case 'S' : Cost = NumberOfLitres * 82.9; break;
   default: WriteStringCr("Type not recognised. Please re-enter transaction.");
 }
 WriteFloatPr("The cost in pence is ", Cost);
```

The default case would attempt to write out an uninitialised *Cost* value. The solution is to insert an initialisation of *Cost* to 0.0 just after the declarations.

Solution 3.7

```
int Index;
AnsiString MyStr;
 MyStr = ReadStringPr("Enter a non-empty string: ");
 Index = Length(MyStr);
 while (Index >= 1)
 {
   WriteChar(MyStr[Index]);
   Index = Index - 1;
 }
```

Solution 3.8

The course team's suggestions would be as follows.

An opening comment to describe the overall purpose of the program would help. This might take two lines:

> // Program to simulate a pocket calculator.
> // Only addition, subtraction, multiplication and division allowed.

(If you were to use the alternative form for long comments, this would become

> /* Program to simulate a pocket calculator. Only addition,
> subtraction, multiplication and division allowed.*/

However, you should keep to one-line comments.)

The choice of initial values was important to start off the calculation. A helpful comment/reminder, at the appropriate point of the design, might be

> // First value of NextVal will become value of Answer.

A reminder that '=' is entered to terminate the loop would not go amiss.

> // Entry of '=' finishes the program.

Finally, a refinement to step 3.2.5 of the design was made to safeguard against division by zero. Although the code is probably self-explanatory, a comment to highlight its purpose does no harm.

> // Division by zero is avoided here.

Solutions to the Computer Activities

Section 1

Solution 1.1

You should have discovered that *ReadIntPr* works by reading the input string as far as the first non-digit (it correctly recognises an initial minus sign as being a permitted part of an integer) and ignoring anything that follows. For example, each of the inputs 23.78 and 23A are interpreted as being the integer 23, and −23.78 is interpreted as −23. When the first character is not a digit or a minus sign, as in the case with input A23, *ReadIntPr* interprets the input as being 0.

When you hit the Enter key to enter the null string, the response is zero, as it is for any completely invalid entry.

ReadFloatPr behaves in an identical way to *ReadIntPr*. It interprets the input 23.78AXX as being 23.78, interprets any input which does not begin with a digit, a decimal point or a minus sign as being zero. The null string also gives zero.

Section 2

For reference, the code body of `ErrProg1U.cpp` is reproduced here. The first four activities all concern this code.

```
int Next;
int Sum;
 Sum = 0;
 Next = 1;
 Target = ReadIntPr("Enter target number: ")
 while (sum <= Target) do
    Sum = Sum + Next;
    Next = Next + 1;
 WriteIntPr("The number needed was ", Next - 1);
```

Solution 2.1

There are two errors and one warning reported. The first message

> [C++ Error]ErrProg1U.cpp(18):E2451 Undefined symbol 'Target'

points to a problem with *Target* on line 18 of `ErrProg1U.cpp`. You should be able to guess what this means: the variable *Target* has not been declared.

The second message

> [C++ Error]ErrProg1U.cpp(19):E2379 Statement missing ;

should have led you to a missing semicolon at the end of line 18.

The third message

> [C++ Warning]ErrProg1U.cpp(25):W8004'Sum' is assigned a value that is never used

is a warning. A compiler warning is not the same thing as a compilation error. The compiler can carry out exactly what it has been told to do, but is reporting to you that something might not be right. In this case it has detected a declared variable *Sum* which the program does not appear to be using. This may seem strange to you as *Sum* does indeed figure in the program. The explanation for this is that the compiler has not been able to sort things out after the earlier missing semicolon, as the next activity will demonstrate.

Solution 2.2

With the declaration of *Target* included and the missing semicolon inserted at the end of (the original) line 18, compilation still fails. What has happened is that the compiler can now fully check the part of the program beyond where the missing semicolon caused problems before. In doing so, it has uncovered two further errors and issued a further warning.

The first error message points to a misspelling in line 20; the variable *Sum* has been given a lower-case 's'.

The second message reveals that something is wrong with the syntax of the **while** loop. What has happened is that the keyword **do** should not be there. There are two types of conditioned loop, namely the **while** loop and the **do while** loop; but this erroneous code has invented a **while do** loop.

The third message is a warning which can be ignored until the foregoing errors have been corrected.

Solution 2.3

With the two further syntax errors corrected, the program compiles successfully. However, something is still wrong! Every run of the program (for any value of *Target*) gives the number of integers needed to exceed *Target* as 1. There is a semantic error, as explained below.

This is one of those hidden errors which if not spotted quickly might prove to be elusive. The body of the **while** loop has two statements, lines 21 and 22, as is emphasised by the indentation. But the braces are missing, and without them the body of the loop consists, by default, of just the first statement. So *Next* is incremented just once, *after* the loop is complete.

The indentation might have made it clear what was intended, but that is not good enough for the compiler. Although the design is semantically correct, the omission at coding of the braces rendered the implementation logically incorrect. It introduced a semantic error. The pair of braces holding the body of the **while** loop is essential when the body involves more than one statement.

Solution 2.4

The program hangs. Because of the missing braces, the loop is now

```
while (Sum <= Target)
   Next = Next + 1;
```

As there is nothing in the loop body which can cause the control condition to change value to **false**, this loops forever with the value of *Next* increasing by 1 at each pass.

To interrupt the program there are several possible methods. One is as follows. Look for a button with the program name on the taskbar. (This is the bar that contains the Start button.) Right-click on that button and choose Close from the popup menu. You will get a box with a message to the effect that the program cannot be closed. Follow whatever instructions you are given in the box to terminate the program.

Another method (which usually works) is simply to click on the cross icon in the top right-hand corner of the program window. This may result in the same message box as the first method, in which case you should respond as before, or the program window may simply close.

A third method is as follows. Click on the Builder button on the taskbar. When Builder reappears, choose Run|Program Reset or press Ctrl+F2.

You may like to finish off this sequence of activities by correcting the code to achieve its purpose, and saving the resulting project.

Solution 2.5

(a) Such a test should reveal no problems.

(b) The program 'raises an exception'. Execution halts, and you get an error message which probably will not make a lot of sense:

> Project ErrProg2.exe raised exception class
>
> EAccessViolation with message 'Access violation at address ***. Read of address ***'. Process stopped. Use Step or Run to continue.

What you will see where we have put '***' depends on the setup of your machine.

This error is caused by your program attempting to access part of memory that does not belong to it. It crops up in a number of situations, a common one being an attempt to access a value via an index but with the index outside the correct range. Here, the program is attempting to write out the character at index 1 of a string which has length 0.

Click on the OK button of the error message window (ignore the advice to 'Use Step or Run to continue') and press Ctrl+F2 to close down the debugger.

(An 'exception' is something generated by the operating system. It signals that the program did something that the protective features of the operating system do not like. Exceptions can be handled by the operating system or the program. Builder gives your programs very basic exception handling facilities automatically.)

Index